The Firestarter Effect

Making Jesus Christ Known
in the Marketplace

Shae Bynes

Antonina D. Geer

Founders, Kingdom Driven Entrepreneur ™

KingdomDrivenEntrepreneur.com

The Firestarter Effect

ISBN 978-0989632256

Copyright 2014 by Kingdom Driven LLC
All rights reserved.

Published by Kingdom Driven Publishing
4846 N. University Drive #406
Lauderhill, FL 33351

Printed in the United States of America

All rights reserved. No portion of this book may be reproduced by any means - electronic, mechanical, photocopy, recording, scanning, or other - except for brief quotations in reviews or articles, without the prior written permission of the publisher. Your support of the authors' rights is appreciated.

Dedication

We dedicate this book to the Kingdom Driven Entrepreneurs who are both ready and willing to be unleashed and see the fullness of God manifested...in themselves and in the marketplace.

Contents

Introduction

As a Kingdom Driven Entrepreneur, you're more than a person in business who has made Jesus Christ your personal Savior. If you're a Kingdom Driven Entrepreneur, your business endeavors are propelled and motivated by the advancement of the Kingdom of God, which is simply God's way of doing things.

You are called by God to the marketplace, and He has given you specific gifts, talents, and abilities and has assigned you specific areas of influence to take territory for the Kingdom of God and see people give their lives to the Lord.

As a Kingdom Driven Entrepreneur, you've yielded your business to God and placed Him as the Ultimate CEO of your business. You're led by the Holy Spirit in your daily operations and you seek Heaven's strategy for your business. You rely on God's way of doing things instead of the world's way of doing things in order to bring unprecedented financial increase through your business that will not only serve your family, but will impact lives globally.

This isn't business as usual.

The Firestarter Effect

This leads us to the purpose of this book *The Firestarter Effect*. Yes, this book is all about starting fires. Your assignment as a Kingdom Driven Entrepreneur is to start fires in the marketplace in the areas that the Lord has called you to. The effect of (or the change that results from) the fires you set ablaze will be territory taken for the Kingdom of God.

At this point, we completely understand if you're scratching your head and asking yourself, "Start fires in the marketplace? What does that mean?" Rest assured that you are in good company because when the Lord spoke to us as the visionaries of the Kingdom Driven Entrepreneur movement and said that we are to be and to activate "Firestarters in the Marketplace", we were scratching our heads as well! However, the Holy Spirit revealed through study of His Word what fire represents and how it applies to us and our businesses as Kingdom Driven Entrepreneurs.

Fire represents God's Presence

There are numerous examples of fire representing the presence of God. In Exodus 3:2, the scripture says "There the angel of the Lord appeared to him in a blazing fire from the middle of a bush. Moses stared in amazement. Though the bush was engulfed in flames, it didn't burn up." Later on in Exodus 13 when Moses led the Israelites out of Egypt, the Lord went ahead of them and guided them during the day by a pillar of cloud and provided light for their journey at night with a pillar of fire.

Fire represents God's Power

In the book of Acts on the day of Pentecost, the scripture talks about how there were flames or tongues of fire that appeared and settled on each of the believers as they gathered. They received an infilling of the Holy Spirit and began to speak in other languages as the Holy Spirit gave them the ability to do so (Acts 2). This was a demonstration of the power of God through His Spirit. Another example is in the book of Jeremiah where the Lord said to Jeremiah, "Is not My Word like fire?" and Jeremiah said that God's Word burned in his heart like fire that was shut up in his bones. It was a fire that he could not contain. He couldn't keep it in. That's the power of Almighty God.

Fire represents God's Passion

In Luke 24:32 when the disciples were in the presence of Jesus, they looked at each other and said, "Did our hearts not burn within us while He talked with us and opened the Scriptures?" What was that? What was the fire that was raging within their hearts? It was passion. It was the love of the Father and the Son.

Fire represents God's Purity

In Malachi 3, the Lord is referred to as a blazing refiner's fire. Malachi 3:3 (New Living Translation) says "He will sit like a refiner of silver, burning away the dross." In 1 Peter, the scripture refers to our faith being tested as fire tests and purifies gold. God is a consuming fire. He is holy and He burns away the impurities within us and refines us to be more like Him.

Being a Firestarter in the Marketplace

Understanding how fire is represented in the Word, we can begin to understand how that pertains to our assignments in the marketplace. In order to start a fire, you have to begin, or set out with intention, to be a demonstrator of God's presence, God's power, God's passion, and God's purity in the marketplace.

By intentionally starting fires in the marketplace, you will make Jesus Christ irresistible to those around you. Your business and your life will speak of the goodness of God. The Apostle Paul says it well in 1 Corinthians 4:20 (The Message): God's Way is not a matter of mere talk; it's an empowered life.

Over these next chapters, we pray that you will be activated to boldly move forward as a Firestarter in the marketplace. Being a Kingdom Driven Entrepreneur is a wild, but an absolutely amazing adventure. Yielding yourself, being in constant pursuit, and allowing the Lord to have free course and authority over your business will yield results exceedingly abundantly above all you could ask or even think according to the power (the Holy Spirit) that works within you (Ephesians 3:20). What you're about to read isn't theory. This is real. The Kingdom of God is at hand.

The Firestarter Formula

If you're going to be effective as a Firestarter -- a demonstrator of God's presence, power, passion, and purity -- there are two key components that you will need to embrace and live out: radical faith and radical obedience.

Radical Faith + Radical Obedience = Fire Ignition

Radical means new and what is different from traditional; it means unusual and extreme. Let's break this formula down:

Radical Faith

It is your faith and belief that activates a response from God. It isn't your fear or insecurities, it is your faith. The Word says that it is impossible to please God without it! Hebrews 11:1 (Amplified) tells us:

> *Now faith is the assurance (the confirmation, the title deed) of the things [we] hope for, being the proof of things [we] do not see and the conviction of their reality [faith perceiving as real fact what is not revealed to these senses].*

Go back and read that again. Read each word and meditate on what it says. When we say that your faith should be radical, we are not referring to being foolish. We are not referring to casting everything aside for the sake of the Gospel without any wisdom or instruction from the Holy Spirit. In fact, Proverbs 1:7 says that it's a fool who despises wisdom and instruction.

Jesus was never foolish. He wasn't a reckless lone ranger. He only did what He saw the Father doing. In John 5:19 Jesus explained, "I tell you the truth, the Son can do nothing by himself. He does only what he sees the Father doing. Whatever the Father, the Son also does."

He knew the Father was exactly who He said He was and it is that faith coupled with the faith of those who encountered him that led to signs, wonders, and miracles. He ignored natural circumstances and did what the Father showed him to do. The Bible is full of stories of individuals who were able to receive the promises of God through Jesus Christ based on their bold faith. They chose to believe rather than to doubt.

When we say it's time for your faith to be radical we mean a new and increased level of faith from where you are right now. As Jesus told the disciples, you only need faith the size of a tiny mustard seed to see God's miracles manifested. If you think about it, He's really not asking that much of us! Commit to new level of faith that is a departure from what has been traditional for you in the past. Faith comes by hearing and hearing by the Word of God, so increase your hearing of the Word. The more you feed your faith with the Word, the greater your expectations will be. You will expect God to move. You will not be surprised when He answers prayer or when signs, wonders, and miracles follow you.

Radical Obedience

The second component to fire ignition for the marketplace is a lifestyle of obedience, or what we like to call A Lifestyle of "Yes." We'll take this a step further and say that it takes more than obedience, but rather it takes *radical obedience*...and that radical obedience will also strengthen your level of faith.

Obedience says "Yes Lord, I'll do that," "Yes Lord, I'm willing," "Yes Lord, I'll go." However, your lifestyle of Yes must be radical. Your "Yes Lord" cannot be based on what makes natural sense to you. It cannot be based on what you've done before or what you're comfortable with -- none of that matters. It doesn't say "Yes Lord, but not right now" when He is clearly telling you to move. Your lifestyle of radical obedience says:

"Lord, that sounds absolutely ludicrous, but Yes Lord I'll do that."

"Lord, I have no idea how I'm going to do that, but Yes Lord, I trust You and I will take the first/next step."

"Lord, the timing for that seems a little odd, but ok...You say now? Let's do it. Yes."

"Lord, are you for real?!? I mean, seriously?!? Ok, whatever You will have me to do. Yes Lord."

"Lord, it's only moments before the event starts and You haven't told me what to say to all these people yet, but Yes Lord, I'll go out there anyway." (We know this one intimately)

Yes. Yes. Yes. Whatever He asks of You, the answer should be "Yes."

Make a Decision and Ignite!

Make a decision today to live a lifestyle of radical faith and radical obedience. Make a decision to view your life and business with your spiritual eyes and ears as opposed to your natural ones. Decide that your personal ambition is worthless unless it is a holy one based purely on obedience to the Lord's will and plan for you. Make a decision to stay in your lane and not add or take away from the vision the Lord gives you for your business. Consider what you've already been instructed to do but haven't done yet, and get busy. Make a decision that if God isn't in it, you're not doing it.

This decision will be a catalyst for some serious fire starting! Not because of who you are, but because of who He is and because of your willingness to be used by Him. Being "radical" with your faith and your obedience is not a badge of honor to boast about and display with pride. Being "radical" is not the goal. Jesus Christ is the goal. A lifestyle of radical faith and radical obedience is a pure hearted decision to live a yielded life, become more like Jesus Christ, and see His name glorified and made great in the Earth.

Now we're ready to talk about how to set some fires ablaze in the marketplace!

****

Need Some Inspiration?

If you're feeling even a little apprehension about this idea of radical faith and radical obedience, we understand. Sometimes it takes hearing about others' experiences to build faith and expectation. This is why testimonies and sharing your story is so important.

If you're feeling a little unsure about this, we encourage you to stop here and go to the Appendix where you will find some awesome Fire Ignition stories that demonstrate the power of this decision. Once you've read those stories, we encourage you to move forward with the remaining chapters of this book. Even if you don't feel the need to stop now and read those stories, we encourage you to read them after you have completed the rest of the book!

****

Demonstrating God's Presence in the Marketplace

"Can anyone hide from me in a secret place? Am I not everywhere in all the heavens and earth?" says the LORD. ~Jeremiah 23:24 (New Living Translation)

There is a good reason why Moses said to the Lord, "If your Presence does not go with us, do not send us up from here" before leading the Israelites to the land God promised. He understood that it was God's presence that made the difference. He knew that it was God's presence that would distinguish them from everyone else on the earth (Exodus 33:15-17).

It was God's presence that brought the blessing for Joseph and caused him to prosper wherever he was. Despite the fact that he suffered at the hands of so many people, was thrown into a pit and sold into slavery, through his obedience he ended up in the king's palace and was successful in every endeavor -- all because of the presence of Almighty God and the blessing (empowerment) that came with Him.

The presence of God brings peace; one that surpasses all understanding and guards your heart and mind (Philippians 4:6-9) independent of your outward circumstances. With the presence of God, you can live without fear because He is greater than anything you face in the world. Yes, the Kingdom of God is righteousness, peace, and joy in the Holy Spirit (Romans 14:17).

God has made YOU a carrier of His presence. You are a carrier of His glory. You are a carrier of His fire. This is true even if you are not called to the office of an apostle, prophet, pastor, teacher, or evangelist in the church. You are a Kingdom Driven Entrepreneur, and God desires to use you mightily in the marketplace to bring His transforming presence. There is an entire world that is hungry and crying out for an encounter with God and to know that He is real. He wants His glory in all the earth.

From Glory to Glory

It is the glory of God, His presence, that changes us and makes us more and more like Him. Meditate on this scripture from 2 Corinthians 3:13-18 (New Living Translation):

> *[13] We are not like Moses, who put a veil over his face so the people of Israel would not see the glory, even though it was destined to fade away. [14] But the people's minds were hardened, and to this day whenever the old covenant is being read, the same veil covers their minds so they cannot understand the truth. And this veil can be removed only by believing in Christ.*
>
> *[15] Yes, even today when they read Moses' writings, their hearts are covered with that veil, and they do not understand.*

[16] But whenever someone turns to the Lord, the veil is taken away. [17] For the Lord is the Spirit, and wherever the Spirit of the Lord is, there is freedom.

[18] So all of us who have had that veil removed can see and reflect the glory of the Lord. And the Lord—who is the Spirit—makes us more and more like him as we are changed into his glorious image.

It's through this process of yielding yourself and being changed into His glorious image, that will cause people to sense the presence of God when they are in your presence regardless of whether they know Jesus Christ or not. He will use you in the most amazing and spontaneous ways to draw people to Him.

Being Aware of His Presence

God is always present and He is everywhere, and before you can demonstrate the presence of God in the marketplace, it's important to cultivate an active awareness of His presence in your personal life. James 4:8 says that as you draw near to God, He will draw near to you. It's about preparing your heart, seeking Him sincerely, and expecting Him to be reveal Himself in the mighty way that He does.

In our devotional *Encountering God: A Devotional for the Kingdom Driven Entrepreneur*, we cover some great ways you can do this in your daily life. Here are a few of them:

- Have conversations with God throughout the day. Just talk to Him like you're talking to a friend. Tell Him what's going on and just listen to what He has to share with you. Those conversations are like prayers.

- Worship Him right in the middle of your work day. Praise Him for who He is in your life and for what He is doing in you, through you, and for you. Pray or even sing in the Holy Spirit. Tell Him how good He is. Not only does He love to hear it, but you will encourage yourself.

- Ask God what He wants! When you're faced with a decision, simply ask Him what to do, what to say, or how to think about a situation. This is something you may already do with large decisions, but try it in smaller matters too. Remember there is no issue too small or too large -- He is concerned with it all.

- Spend quiet time in the mornings or evenings just soaking in the presence of God, listening to some of your favorite worship music and just spending time together. Open your heart to Him and allow Him to minister to your spirit.

The truth is that whatever you are hungry for when it comes to God, He will satisfy it. The more He satisfies that hunger, the hungrier you will get. It's an awesome cycle. Expect God to respond to you. Expect His presence to transform you from the inside out.

Manifestations of God's Presence in the Marketplace

As a carrier of God's fire, there are a number of ways that His transforming presence can be known through your business. Carefully note that none of this requires quoting scriptures, pulling out your Bible, placing a fish symbol on your company van, anointing your customers with oil, or wearing your favorite "I love Jesus" t-shirt or accessory while you're conducting business.

Be a Thermostat

Firestarters set atmospheres and shift undesirable atmospheres. When it comes to setting atmospheres, understand that you are able to create an atmosphere that ushers in the presence and the peace of God; unspeakable peace that those who walk into the room and don't know the love of Christ don't even understand. They simply think to themselves "There's something different about this place" or "It's so peaceful here" or perhaps they don't think anything at all, but their spirit responds to His presence which creates a desirable experience while doing business with you. You never know when someone who is having a terrible day or is going through a very challenging season of life will be impacted by even 5-10 minutes of God's peace in your establishment.

If you're hosting an event, you can set the atmosphere in that room before the attendees show up. If you spend time on the phones with clients, you can set the atmosphere for your call prior to picking up the phone. If you have a business meeting, you can set the atmosphere for that meeting before it even begins.

You can set the atmosphere through prayer, praise, worship (with or without music), and/or declaring the Word of God. Remember that when you draw near to God, He draws near to you. He is drawn to your heart and attention towards Him.

You can also shift atmospheres from undesirable to desirable. You're a carrier of the presence of Almighty God! Did someone walk in the room with a negative attitude before an important meeting was about to begin? Shift the atmosphere! Did you enter someone else's business where the air was so thick and heavy? Be a Firestarter and shift the atmosphere! It doesn't have to be loud or obvious to anyone else -- just shift it!

Your Work is Worship

Did you realize that when you are doing what the Lord has called you to do in business that your work is worship, brings glory to Him, and ushers in the presence of God? The reason it is important to understand this is because sometimes Kingdom Driven Entrepreneurs try too hard to evangelize or make something happen when really they just need to do their work!

Particularly if you're in a service-based business, understand that as you're yielded to the Holy Spirit and invite Him into your business by seeking His direction and strategy for the individual clients you serve, your interactions with your clients and customers are demonstrating the presence of God. You're speaking life and light into their situations. You are solving their problems under the leading of the Holy Spirit. YOU are a carrier of His presence.

It may seem as though we're frowning on the idea of sharing Jesus Christ more overtly, but before you continue to read, we want you to know that cannot be further from the truth. While in many cases, experiencing God and the love of Jesus Christ trumps simply hearing about it, what is most important is that you trust and yield to whatever the Holy Spirit leads and guides you to do in your interactions with others. Timing is important and only the Lord knows whether your role is to plant a seed or to water it.

Activate Presence:

- Cultivate an active awareness of the presence of God in your own personal life.

- Ask the Lord to help you see what He sees and to increase your awareness of the needs of people around you.

- Set the atmosphere in your business on a regular basis -- not as a religious ritual, but as a God-pleasing and honoring activity because you love Him and want to make His presence known.

Demonstrating God's Power in the Marketplace

But you shall receive power (ability, efficiency, and might) when the Holy Spirit has come upon you, and you shall be My witnesses in Jerusalem and all Judea and Samaria and to the ends (the very bounds) of the earth.
~Acts 1:8 (Amplifed)

Where God is present, so is His power. To say God is a master strategist is an understatement. He gave you the Holy Spirit to abide on the inside of you the moment you accepted Jesus Christ as your personal Savior, but He also gave you the power, ability, and might to do His work in the earth through the baptism of the Holy Spirit. It is not your might or your power, but that of the Holy Spirit.

The Holy Spirit Within and Upon

If you are truly going to be a Firestarter in the marketplace, it's vitally important to not only embrace the Holy Spirit within you (1 Corinthians 6:19, John 14:16), but to also embrace the Holy Spirit upon you.

The Holy Spirit living on the inside of you is what enables you to produce fruit. Through the Holy Spirit indwelling you're empowered to produce love, joy, peace, patience (long suffering), kindness, goodness, faithfulness, gentleness, and self-control. This is clearly important for doing business God's way, operating your business in excellence and with integrity. That is the Holy Spirit *within you.*

The Holy Spirit *upon you* is for service. Jesus told the disciples that they would receive power after the Holy Spirit came upon them (Acts 1:8) and that they would be endued with power from on high (Luke 24:49). Why? To do the works of the Father. There are gifts from the Holy Spirit that are manifestations of God's power -- some of these gifts do, some speak, and others reveal, but they all serve as ministry. As a Kingdom Driven Entrepreneur, your business is ministry.

Manifestations of God's Power

The Apostle Paul talks about nine gifts of the Holy Spirit in 1 Corinthians 12:7-10 and each of these gifts represents a manifestation of the power of God. While there are arguably more than nine spiritual gifts discussed throughout the Bible, we're going to focus our attention on this passage of scripture:

> *A spiritual gift is given to each of us so we can help each other. To one person the Spirit gives the ability to give wise advice; to another the same Spirit gives a message of special knowledge. The same Spirit gives great faith to another, and to someone else the one Spirit gives the gift of healing. He gives one person the power to perform miracles, and another the ability to prophesy. He gives someone else the ability to discern whether a message is from the Spirit of God or from another spirit. Still another person*

> *is given the ability to speak in unknown languages, while another is given the ability to interpret what is being said. (1 Corinthians 12:7-10, New Living Translation)*

We can categorize these in 3 ways: gifts that do things (gift of faith, healing, miracles), gifts that speak things (prophecy, speaking in tongues, interpretation of tongues) , and gifts that reveal things (word of wisdom, word of knowledge, discerning of spirits).

You have some (and potentially even all) of these gifts. As the Apostle Paul said, each believer is given a gift (or gifts) so that we can be of service to others. These are gifts of the Holy Spirit which means you cannot earn them and you cannot boast in them. While these gifts are for the Body of Christ, they should not be confined to the four walls of a church building. These gifts empower us to do the work of Jesus Christ...yes, in the marketplace too!

We won't go into extensive detail of each of these gifts (we encourage you to do your own study), but it's important for us to discuss how some of these gifts can and do manifest in the marketplace.

Manifestations of God's Power in the Marketplace

You may have experienced a manifestation of God's power in your business before -- with or without recognizing it as such. Here are a few examples:

Word of Knowledge

A word of knowledge is information revealed to you (from God through the Holy Spirit) that you otherwise wouldn't have known on your own. It could come from an inward revelation, a dream, a vision, through the Word of God, or through other means.

There are many instances of Word of Knowledge in the Bible, and one powerful example is with Jesus ministering to the Samaritan woman at the well (John 4:13-19).

> *[13] Jesus replied, "Anyone who drinks this water will soon become thirsty again. [14] But those who drink the water I give will never be thirsty again. It becomes a fresh, bubbling spring within them, giving them eternal life."*
> *[15] "Please, sir," the woman said, "give me this water! Then I'll never be thirsty again, and I won't have to come here to get water."*
> *[16] "Go and get your husband," Jesus told her.*
> *[17] "I don't have a husband," the woman replied. Jesus said, "You're right! You don't have a husband— [18] for you have had five husbands, and you aren't even married to the man you're living with now. You certainly spoke the truth!" [19] "Sir," the woman said, "you must be a prophet.*

As a result of this encounter, this woman's life was transformed and there was a spiritual revival in her village. The people begged Jesus to stay in their village and in a matter of two days many in the village became believers.

If you're in a business where you work directly one on one with people (such as coaching counseling, and consulting), think of how powerful this gift can be in your business for your clients. When you speak into the lives of others and the Holy Spirit gives you deeper insight into the other person, this can bring supernatural transformation to the lives of those you serve. If the Holy Spirit reveals to you, be bold about following His leading on what to do with that knowledge revealed as you're serving through your business.

Word of Wisdom

A word of wisdom is much like a word of knowledge except that not only do you receive insight into specific people or situations, but you also receive an understanding of what to do with that insight and how to do it. It's not just the ability to see/hear the "what" but also the "how." There are things the Lord will give you wisdom on that there is absolutely no way your skills or experience could have provided it.

A powerful example in the Bible is with King Solomon (1 Kings 3:16-28). Two prostitutes came to King Solomon to have an argument settled regarding a baby. Both women had a baby within days of each other and one of the babies died. Each woman was claiming that the surviving baby belonged to them. In a divinely inspired moment, King Solomon comes up with a seemingly crazy suggestion: "Bring me a sword! Cut the living child into two, and give half to one woman and half to the other!" One woman cried out "Oh no, my lord! Give her the child -- please do not kill him!" while the other woman said "All right, he will be neither yours nor mine; divide him between us!" That settled it. The king rendered justice and proclaimed that the baby belonged to the woman who loved the child enough to see him live because clearly she was his mother. King Solomon received both divine insight and strategy for handling the situation.

Through godly wisdom, you will be able to solve problems at a greater level and perhaps solve problems in areas that you have absolutely no natural ability in. Similarly to a word of knowledge, experiencing this revelatory gift can be powerful for people who serve as coaches, counselors, or consultants. The Lord may give you the wisdom on how to apply God's Word to the practical matters of life for those you serve. He'll give you a specific word at a specific time for a specific person. When you deliver that word, it will likely not be best delivered in the King James Version! It will sound more like the New Living Translation or The Message, particularly when speaking with non-believers. The chapter and verse isn't the most important thing, the word of God is....and it's power.

It is also possible that you will create entire products or services completely through a word of wisdom. Alicia Hommon, CEO of Cake Whimzy in St.

Louis, Missouri, makes custom cakes for a variety of clients and occasions. She shared that while she has baking talent, she doesn't have any natural artistic talent for designing these intricately detailed cakes. When she gets an order from a client, she sits down and waits for the Holy Spirit to download the entire design and process for making the cake through a dream. She won't start an order before getting that wisdom. Isn't that powerful?

Prophecy

The gift of prophecy is a divinely inspired message revealing the will of God. The act of prophesying is the act of speaking this message under the inspiration of the Holy Spirit, discerning what it is that the Lord wants to have shared at that time for that person or group of people. It can be predictive, but can also be a speaking forth of God's Word. A prophetic word can serve to strengthen, encourage, and comfort (1 Corinthians 14:3), and can also bring conviction (1 Corinthians 14:24-25) to those who hear, drawing them to Christ.

You don't have to walk in the spiritual office of a prophet in order for the Lord to give a prophetic word for you to speak to someone you encounter in business. The Bible provides examples of people who were not prophets, but were used to bring a prophetic word. King Saul was used mightily by God and prophesied along with all of the schooled prophets (1 Samuel 10:10-13).

Be courageous and if the Holy Spirit is prompting you to speak, whether it be for an audience at your event, a customer, a business partner, or employee, do it! You don't even have to say that the Lord told you to say it. Speak what the Holy Spirit gives you to speak and allow God to do what He does so well and speak to the heart of the person (or people) on the receiving end. Many well-meaning believers make the mistake of believing that a word cannot be delivered without adding "Thus saith the Lord." You're in the marketplace, not within a church building. Simply yield yourself and speak.

Healing

You don't have to be in a medical, massage, or health and nutrition-related business to be used to bring supernatural healing to others. Those are surely industries to see God's miracle working power in action, but God is not limited so neither are you.

Saxophonist Jordan Chalden has seen the Lord bring healing to people's physical bodies through listening to his music! The Lord has anointed him with a gift to set an atmosphere that activates faith and produces miracles. When we had our first Kingdom Driven Entrepreneur Retreat in Phoenix, Arizona, deliverance and healing took place all weekend....at a business Retreat (and you can read more of the story in the Appendix of this book)!

Not Business As Usual

We encourage you to truly embrace these manifestations and yield yourself completely to them. It is an honor to be used by God....an absolute honor! Make yourself available, be sensitive to the leading of the Holy Spirit and operate out of a place of love for others.

Remember that Kingdom driven entrepreneurship is not business as usual. While many business owners (Christian or otherwise) may find all of this a bit crazy, this is the life of a Firestarter. As a Firestarter, you allow yourself to be used mightily and even in unusual ways to see lives impacted and Jesus Christ glorified.

Activate Power:

- If there are gifts of the Holy Spirit that you do not understand, begin a self-study on these gifts asking the Lord to guide you to truth and give you understanding.

- Have a willing heart to be used by God in your business. Imagine if Alicia Hommon ignored her calling to design cakes because she didn't have a natural skill for it?

- Embrace the notion that no gift is greater than the other. Cast down any thoughts of envy or inadequacy based on the gifts that you see others operating in.

- Expect to receive godly wisdom. Expect it in unprecedented ways. You never know how the Lord is going to use you in the marketplace.

- Before meetings, ask the Lord for doors to be opened for His power to be made known.

- Don't be sloppy with spiritual gifts. If you receive a word of knowledge regarding someone you encounter through business, ask the Lord to reveal the purpose. Is it for you to pray about privately? Is it to be shared with the individual? If you're in a public setting (an event or meeting), be sure that if the word is going to be spoken that it is edifying.

Demonstrating God's Passion in the Marketplace

God is love, and all who live in love live in God, and God lives in them. And as we live in God, our love grows more perfect. So we will not be afraid on the day of judgment, but we can face him with confidence because we live like Jesus here in this world. ~ 1 John 4:16-17

God is love and everything that He does is motivated by His love for you. His love is intense and extravagant. It is perfect and boundless -- it is without restrictions or conditions. His love cannot increase or decrease for you. It never runs out. He is jealous for you. His love cannot be any more fervent, heated, or intense than it is right now.

This love we're talking about extends to every person on the planet, and absolutely nothing can separate you from it. That is the love of God. It is fire.

You love because He first loved you.

Your capacity to love others and to be a demonstrator of God's passion in the marketplace is directly tied to your capacity to understand the love that God has for you. That understanding will also help you to fully trust God to be everything that He says He is, to do everything that He says He will do (or has already done), and also to purify your love so that you're able to pour lovingly into the lives of others you encounter in your business -- even the people who would ordinarily be hard to love.

The transformation that happens within you as you understand and embrace how great His love is for you will help you see people the way God sees them. It will help you to see past their faults, their idiosyncrasies, rude behavior, or other irritations. It will help you respond differently and not always take things personally.

Manifestations of God's Passion in the Marketplace

In 1 Corinthians 13:4-7, the Apostle Paul gives us a hint on how we can demonstrate the love of God in the marketplace:

> *Love is patient, love is kind. It does not envy, it does not boast, it is not proud. It does not dishonor others, it is not self-seeking, it is not easily angered, it keeps no record of wrongs. Love does not delight in evil but rejoices with the truth. It always protects, always trusts, always hopes, always perseveres.*

Each of these is a choice. It is an expression of your will and intention and it can be applied to prospects, customers/clients, employees, and business partners.

For God so loved the world, He GAVE.

While the Apostle Paul provides solid insight that will help you to walk in love towards others, the most quoted scripture in the Bible, John 3:16, best exemplifies how to demonstrate God's love: For God loved the world so much that He gave His one and only Son, so that everyone who believes in Him will not perish but have everlasting life (New Living Translation).

If you follow the model of your Heavenly Father, you will be compelled to give, and to give radically. Radical means "extreme, unusual, different from the norm, and aggressive." God loved us so radically that He gave the entire world His only son Jesus to redeem us. Often times as entrepreneurs we focus on the importance of being wildly passionate about the product or service we provide, but to be a Firestarter in the marketplace you need to be radically passionate about *the people you serve and the people who serve you.* That radical love is expressed through your radical giving.

There are countless applications of this in a business context, but let's explore some ways that you can express radical love through radical giving in your business:

Radical Sowing

Sowing your products and services into the lives of others is a wonderful way to express love. It's best to be led by the Holy Spirit in your giving because it will keep you from overdoing the giving to the detriment of your profitability. Additionally, when you allow the Holy Spirit to guide you and you yield to His promptings, your otherwise random acts of kindness become strategic acts of kindness which yield supernatural results (for you and others) that you simply could not have pre-determined.

Alicia Williams is a hair stylist and she shared how she asks the Lord to reveal one person she should sow into each week by giving them their salon service at no charge. Candace Ford, CEO of Nibrima Branding & Design shared how the Holy Spirit will at times prompt her to sow her branding and design services to clients. For example, her recent obedience to complete a logo design at no charge for a non-profit organization led to an unanticipated outcome when the organization was able to secure celebrity sponsorship to help pay all the travel and medical costs for a very ill child on the other side of the world to receive life saving surgery and treatment -- a life forever impacted because an organization was able to confidently present a professional image.

When we were preparing for our first Kingdom Driven Entrepreneur national Retreat in Phoenix, Arizona, the Lord led us to provide highly discounted registrations to select individuals. We didn't choose the recipients, He did. Not only did He choose the recipients, but He gave us the provision to do it through the generosity of others both within and outside of the Kingdom Driven Entrepreneur community. It was through that giving that a number of people were able to attend and experience a life-changing encounter with God and make divine connections that will lead to unprecedented results in their respective marketplace assignments. God's ways are higher than our ways and His thoughts are higher than our thoughts.

Radical Appreciation

Can you imagine the fires you can start by simply creating a culture of radical appreciation in your business -- appreciation to prospective clients for the mere consideration of your services, appreciation to current customers, appreciation to your employees (or contractors), and appreciation to your business partners?

There are many ways to do this. For example, you can allocate 2-4 hours each month towards phone calls or personal handwritten letters to express appreciation to them and (optionally) bless them with an additional surprise gift. This doesn't have to cost much, and rest assured that when you involve the Lord in this, all provision for what He leads will be made available to you.

Truly listen when you're having conversations with people you encounter in business. Discover what they like, what they dislike, what they need, what they desire. When you listen and observe, you'll find that conversations will leave clues. Those clues help you to personalize how you express your appreciation in such a manner that the person on the receiving end is moved by your unusual demonstration of love -- it will model how Your Father cares about every single detail concerning you.

Hugs

Yes, hugs. When you are filled with love of God and you hug another individual (not with one of those annoying and impersonal half hugs that are really more like a pat on the back, but a REAL hug), they are a recipient of that love. The love of Jesus Christ that someone encounters from you can change and even heal their heart. You cannot underestimate what supernaturally takes place through what seems to be ordinary natural contact.

The Holy Spirit will help you to discern when it may be inappropriate to do so, but as a general rule you should open yourself up to physical forms of love expression with those you encounter through your business. That physical expression may be a hug, but it could also be as simple as a touch on the shoulder, arm, or hand. Don't misinterpret this to mean that you need to go around hugging everyone. This is about willingness and openness to do as you're led to do so.

Not Quite Perfect, But Being Perfected

Jesus told his disciples (John 13:35) that they would be known by the love they display towards each other. You will also be known for how you love. In order to draw others to Christ, they need to see a manifestation, or demonstration, of His love.

It's important to recognize that while your love walk is not perfect right now, it is being perfected through Him as you spend time in His presence and demonstrate love towards others (1 John 4:12). Pray that your eyes will be opened to His wondrous love in ways you haven't seen or experienced before. Seek God and ask the Holy Spirit to increase your capacity to receive more of His love and to demonstrate His love to others. He will be faithful to do it.

Activate Love:

- Spend time daily with the Lord who is the lover of your soul. It is your most important business meeting of the day.

- Whenever you're feeling stressed or irritated by a situation you're facing with an individual you're dealing with in your life or business, take a moment to worship. This doesn't require music and it doesn't require much time. It is a matter of your heart and what you express through it. Worship provides proper perspective!

- Take inventory of how you're currently expressing (or have previously expressed) radical love through your business. What fires were started and what were the results?

- Commit to a lifestyle of radical giving through your business and seek God on specific strategy for you.

Demonstrating God's Purity in the Marketplace

But now you must be holy in everything you do, just as God who chose you is holy. For the Scriptures say, "You must be holy because I am holy." ~ 1 Peter 1:15-16 (New International Version)

Living a holy life is the beginning of demonstrating God's purity in the marketplace. In the Bible, Peter reminds us that in everything we do we must be holy. Why must we be holy, set apart, and devoted to God in the marketplace? Because God is holy! As Firestarters who are representatives of Jesus Christ in the marketplace, we must strive to live holy as Jesus did and exhibit purity and light in business.

A Remnant of Firestarters

The ultimate mission of a follower of Jesus Christ is to "go and make disciples" (Matthew 28:19, New King James Version). This is what scholars call the Great Commission. As a Kingdom Driven Entrepreneur, this is the ultimate reason why you have been called into business. Yes, being in business brings financial increase so that you can take care of your family and give to others. However there is an even greater purpose -- God desires that all would be saved and come into the knowledge of Christ, making Him known in the marketplace.

He has called you to be holy and set apart for a specific purpose of influence and impact in business so that people in the marketplace who otherwise wouldn't attend a church gathering or service are drawn to Him and accept Jesus Christ as their personal Savior. Unfortunately, we live in a world that has a tarnished view of Christianity as a result of many who wear the title of Christian, but are not living a submitted life to Christ.

However that is shifting as God is preparing a remnant of people -- Firestarters who have pure hearts and the desire to please Him in life and in business. He's elevating a people who have been called to minister not just in words, but through their day to day living. As a Firestarter you will change the way the marketplace views Christianity by setting ablaze the fire of God's purity in business through living a holy life before those you serve, partner with, and meet through business endeavors.

God's Refining Fire

One of the oldest methods of refining metals is refining by flame. Through the refinement process, the gold is melted and the dross, or unwanted impurities, rises to the top of the molten metal and is skimmed off. The result? A purified gold.

This is the analogy that God used when speaking through the prophet Zechariah (Zechariah 13:9, New Living Translation):

> *I will bring that group through the fire and make them pure.*
>
> *I will refine them like silver and purify them like gold.*
>
> *They will call on my name,and I will answer them.*
>
> *I will say, 'These are my people,' and they will say, 'The LORD is our God.'"*

Perhaps it sounds painful, and it is to the flesh, but if we're to be a set apart people who represent Jesus Christ, it's a necessary and beneficial process. When you lay down your will, thoughts, heart, and life at the feet of Jesus, God will refine and purify you. He will burn anything that is unlike Him. In the process of doing so, you're able to be a true ambassador of Christ and make His name great in the marketplace.

2 Timothy 2:20-21 in the New Living Translation makes it really plain and explains that in wealthy home there are some utensils made of gold and silver and some made of wood and clay. The expensive ones are used for special occasions, while the cheap ones are for everyday use. When you allow the Lord to purify you, you live a life that is clean -- a special utensil for honorable use -- and you're ready to be used by the Lord for every good work.

When you've been purified it will show up in the way you respond to those you work with. It will be evident in situations when there's a point of decision to be made to choose God's way or to compromise. When you've been refined in God's fire, it will also manifest in your character. That light of Christ in you will cause some who may not know Him to notice there's something different about you, ask questions, and open the door for you to share the Gospel and introduce the God you serve.

Manifestations of God's Purity in the Marketplace

Who you are and how you show up in business is key to demonstrating God's purity in business.

Let Your Character Speak for You

One of the most effective ways of being a witness of Jesus Christ is living in a way in which your character shows that you know Him. Instead of talking the talk, you walk it out being a living epistle -- a manifestation of Jesus being in your life. Often times, people will first see your personality, your honesty, your behavior, the choices you make, your actions, and your response to them and situations before they will hear your words. Who you are speaks more loudly than what you say.

Every day in business presents opportunities or challenges for you to respond as Jesus Christ would in a situation. Be consistent in the way you treat people, always being respectful regardless of how someone treats you.

Be a person of integrity in your business dealings by following through on what you say you will deliver for clients, customers, or partners. Be a Kingdom Driven Entrepreneur who strives for excellence in character and in skill, producing quality work for those you serve.

Tell Your Story

You have a story. You may have been through tests in life that were painful and difficult. These tests served as sanctification for you and you experienced God's transforming work within you. People need to hear your story of how Jesus Christ has changed your life.

In business as you nurture and build relationships, you will find that there are occasions when you are compelled to be transparent about your life to someone. Your transparency may reveal your own personal life's struggles, weaknesses, and will show that even though you are Christian you're not perfect. You can also share the triumphs in your life, the great experiences that had nothing to do with your goodness, but had everything to do with God moving in your life.

It is in the telling of your story that people will begin to trust you and open up to you, and can open doors to share that in the same way Christ has changed you, He can change them.

Activate Purity:

- Develop a holy lifestyle by submitting to God's purification in your life and live to please Him.

- Understand and embrace the fact that sometimes the Lord will call you to put aside something that you do and enjoy. Often times it's not that what you're doing is a "sin" but it's because He wants your heart and attention towards Him. He is working on you! Yield to that instruction.

- Pray this prayer or a similar prayer: "Lord my heart is to please you, I yield my life to you, purify me so that I can be useful for Your work in the marketplace."

- Be attentive to the Holy Spirit promptings while working in business, and the opportunities He presents for you to share your story and introduce Christ to someone.

Ready to Ignite?

You may be thinking "Wait a second...we didn't talk much about making money in all this fire starting! Isn't that the cornerstone of entrepreneurship?" This isn't a book for Christians who happen to be in business. This is a book for Kingdom Driven Entrepreneurs who truly have a heart to see Jesus Christ known in the marketplace. Here's an important truth for you to receive as a Kingdom Driven Entrepreneur: when you make the Father's business a cornerstone of your business, money will not be your concern.

Remember Matthew 6:33?

> *Seek the Kingdom of God above all else, and live righteously, and he will give you everything you need (New Living Translation).*

Yes, God will provide for every work He has called you to. He will bring the divine connections. He will open doors of opportunity. He will close doors that need to be closed. He will keep and protect you. He will add supernaturally to what you put your hands to naturally to bring more clients, more ideas to implement, whatever it is that you need to accomplish the assignment. He's a God of multiplication and yes He desires for your business to be thriving and profitable.

You simply need to give him a "Yes" and act like you mean it (through your faithful action)!

We pray that this book has ignited a hunger to be a Firestarter and make Jesus Christ irresistible in the marketplace. Let your fire burn 24/7. While you won't always "feel" the fire raging inside of you all day, be aware that you have the very Spirit of God flowing on the inside of you. Simply having awareness will allow you to be led by Him as a demonstrator of His presence, His power, His passion, and His purity in the marketplace.

Your fire starting isn't only going to draw unbelievers to Christ, but it will also set believers who are bound by religion free. Your fire starting will lead to believers re-dedicating their lives to Christ and truly encountering God for the first time in their lives. To top it all off, your fire starting is also going to increase your faith, draw you even closer to your Heavenly Father, and provide the most amazing adventure of your life. God in His infinite wisdom and boundless love leaves absolutely nothing out.

We encourage you to go forth with boldness because as a Kingdom Driven Entrepreneur you are well equipped to be a Firestarter in the marketplace. Philippians 4:13 in the Amplified Bible says is well:

> *You have strength in all things in Christ who empowers you. You are ready for anything and equal to anything through Him who infuses inner strength into you. You are self-sufficient in Christ's sufficiency.*

Now get out there and ignite the marketplace to glory of God!

Shae Bynes & Antonina Geer
Founders, Kingdom Driven Entrepreneur
Activating Firestarters in the Marketplace
KingdomDrivenEntrepreneur.com

Join our online community free at
http://KingdomDrivenEntrepreneur.com/community

Appendix: Fire Ignition Stories

We're so glad you have decided to read some awesome stories (as told by the passionate storyteller of the duo, Shae Bynes) of the goodness of God and the fire ignition that has taken for the Kingdom Driven Entrepreneur movement as a result of radical faith and radical obedience.

We pray that the stories on the following pages will inspire you to boldly push forward in whatever the Lord has called you to do and yield yourself to the leading and instruction of the Holy Spirit, no matter how unusual the instructions are. God's way is the best way. It's His way that results in exceedingly, abundantly above all you could ask or even think.

The Birth of Kingdom Driven Entrepreneur

It was spring 2012 and my friend and fellow real estate entrepreneur Steve reached out to me and said "Shae, you absolutely have to meet this woman Lisa." He said we'd really hit it off and that we had so much in common. In fact, he said we even reminded him of each other. Naturally, I agreed to have him connect the two of us and he did. I hopped on the phone with Lisa and we had a nice chat. We had a few things in common and she seemed like a great person, but for the life of me I couldn't figure out why Steve was so adamant about us meeting. The connection didn't quite match his level of enthusiasm or urgency.

To this day we laugh about this because he couldn't even explain why he felt so strongly about us meeting. We now know that it was simply a holy burden.

At the end of my chat with Lisa she told me that I had to meet one of her coaching clients, Antonina Geer. She said that she was absolutely brilliant and that we'd really hit it off. I figured "Hey, why not?" so I connected with Antonina on Facebook, we exchanged a couple messages, and scheduled a time to chat.

On March 22, 2012, Antonina and I had our first phone call and spoke for 2 hours. We were definitely kindred spirits! We talked about business, family, our journey in entrepreneurship, and even talked about the things that we believed the Lord called us to that we hadn't started to do yet. I remember telling her about a couple things the Lord had been speaking to me about transitioning to something that more overtly promotes the merging of faith and business....and I distinctly remember saying "But that's not for now...that's probably 2 or 3 years out." Antonina later told me that when I said that she immediately heard in her spirit "No, that's not for 2 or 3 years out" and that it was going to be way sooner than I thought.

We recognized an opportunity to do something to help each others' audiences, so I led a training for her coaching clients and she was a guest on my podcast to share tips on business finances. We did that over the next couple of weeks, but after it was over there was still a sense that there was another reason why we met. We agreed to pray about it and meet back together in a week. We spoke on the phone again and discussed some ideas, but none of them sounded right. We decided to go pray again and come back. On the third round, Antonina said the words "Kingdom Driven Entrepreneur" and my spirit leapt! I said something like "That's it! That's it! It's a community....it's a movement and it starts with a book." It was a completely divine and masterfully orchestrated moment.

Over the next hour, we outlined our entire first book *The Kingdom Driven Entrepreneur: Doing Business God's Way*. Antonina had never written a book, and I had written only one e-book. We divided up the writing work, and went off on our individual ways to write. When we exchanged our first chapters with each other we were blown away. Our chapters read very similarly -- from the same spirit as if the same person wrote them. We continued to write and exchange chapters throughout late summer and early fall of 2012.

When the book was completed, we decided that it would be nice to meet face to face before launching it and starting a community. We signed an operating agreement and created a business and really didn't know all that the Lord had in store. Antonina flew down to Fort Lauderdale and we had a wonderful time. While we were together for those few days, the Lord confirmed our direction to start a community using our book. We launched the book in November as a free Kindle download, hit the Amazon best-seller list with over 2,000 downloads, and started a community of over 500 people in 3 days. It was all rather surreal.

We didn't even know what we were supposed to do after that. We only had two instructions: write and release the book and start a community. It wasn't until we were radically obedient to take that step that the Lord began to reveal more for us to do.

Here we are now, 16 months later (at the time of the publishing of this book), with 8 published books including 3 Amazon best-sellers, a well-received weekly podcast with over 7,000 downloads, a global online community, a successful national Retreat, and Kingdom Driven Entrepreneur small groups launching all over the globe.

Only God. Not only did the Lord bring two complete strangers together to start a movement to make Jesus Christ known in the marketplace and facilitate divine connections, but He also gave me the best friend, sister, and partner I could ever ask for. We take absolutely no credit for any of this, because it's all God and He deserves all of the glory for what He has done and for all that is to come through this Kingdom Driven Entrepreneur movement. What we have seen has been awesome, but we haven't seen anything yet. We are absolutely honored to be given this assignment for the marketplace. We are honored to be asked and we are honored to now and forever say "Yes Lord!"

Nothing But Covenant

God birthed an awesome covenant partnership and friendship between Antonina and I through Kingdom Driven Entrepreneur, but He also blessed us with an amazing group of brothers and sisters to be a covering, support, and source of wise and godly counsel. At a time when Antonina and I were beginning to talk about the idea of having an Advisory Board for our business, the Lord gave us something substantially better. The Holy Spirit specifically gave me the words "Covenant Board" during a dream and showed me four names and faces the next day while walking my dog in the neighborhood.

What's interesting is that we had never heard of a Covenant Board. In fact, while perhaps they may exist, we are yet to hear of any other business or organization having one. Covenant is a commitment and responsibility not to be taken lightly. With covenant there is unconditional love and a deliberate loyalty and commitment. Covenant is not seasonal; it endures. It's just not your ordinary friendship nor your ordinary advisory board.

What is interesting about the people the Lord gave us for our Covenant Board is that we barely knew them. At the time we couldn't tell you how many kids they had, what their spouses names were, how long they had been in business....really if we had to take a quiz on any of them, we probably would've failed the quiz. Nevertheless, we worked on a list of responsibilities and expectations and invited each of them to join our Covenant Board.

They all said yes and were honored to do it. Just a couple steps of radical obedience needed from us and now these 4 people have become very close friends as well as both a spiritual and naturally covering for our business. They are people whose desires we have taken on as our own and each of them treats Kingdom Driven Entrepreneur as if it was their own business, even though they have businesses of their own. We could not have picked these people ourselves. In fact, we wouldn't have chosen them because of the newness of our relationship. When you yield yourself to the Holy Spirit's instruction, the results are always infinitely better than what you could do on your own.

Covenant has been an integral part of this journey of the Kingdom Driven Entrepreneur movement. It will be key for you in your individual journey as well. Not only covenant with your spouse (if you're married), but covenant with others outside of your natural family. It's such an important concept to understand and embrace that we are releasing a Kingdom Driven Entrepreneur Guide on covenant in Spring 2014.

Shout out to the Kingdom Driven Entrepreneur Covenant Board: David Burrus, Candace Ford, Alicia Hommon, and Alex Navas. We love you all very much and are extraordinarily blessed to have you all in our lives. Thank you!

Phoenix Fire

"So....I have been trying to answer the famous question from friends and family "How was the KDE Retreat"? Needless to say, I have been failing miserably. There is no earthy language sophisticated enough to describe what transpired at the event. It was indeed a 21st century "Day of Pentecost" new birth experience for marketplace leaders.

We were all with one accord, with one mind, with one spirit, in one place, in high expectation, waiting on the promises of God, with cloven tongues of fire resting upon us, listening to audible sounds from Heaven, dwelling in the presence and power of the Holy Spirit - witnessing signs, miracles, revelations, and wonders all around us.

I am still in complete and utter awe and amazement. Grateful that God chose me to be a Kingdom Driven Entrepreneur!"

These are the words of one of our attendees from our first national event, the Kingdom Driven Entrepreneur Retreat in Phoenix, Arizona on January 24-26, 2014. The words above don't sound like a description of a business retreat, but it absolutely was -- a business retreat that through radical faith and radical obedience was an indescribable encounter with God. His manifested presence met us there that weekend. People were healed, delivered, restored, reaffirmed, and repositioned.

Divine connections were made through powerful mastermind sessions where every question was answered and every resource requested was met. Radical giving took place. We saw people experience harvests on their seeds sown within hours. One attendee received a supernatural harvest on a seed that she hadn't even sown yet! She had only said "Yes Lord" to the instruction to sow and received a harvest on it before she could get to the bank to get the money she was sowing!

"You do the logistics with excellence. I will handle the rest."

The planning process for the Retreat was an interesting experience. Antonina and I put together a schedule and a loose draft of an agenda. We knew we had to communicate some kind of agenda so we did the best we could and made sure to include a disclaimer that said "agenda is subject to change." Week after week as we were getting closer to the event, we were seeking God about content for the agenda. We had questions! *How are we going to prepare for them, Lord? Don't we need to create some charts or something? What are we doing? What do you want us to teach about?*

Whenever I was sitting in my bed chatting with God about the Retreat agenda, His responses to my questions were always about logistics. The Holy Spirit would remind me of things we needed to do, but hadn't even thought of yet. Multiple times in the middle of prayer, I experienced visions about the Retreat, but when I asked the Lord to help me to understand the details of what was happening in those very brief visions, He still wanted to talk about logistics! Whenever Antonina would seek the Lord about the agenda, He'd simply tell her not to worry about it because the attendees were coming to encounter Him.

It was three weeks before the Retreat and we still didn't know what was going to take place in three different time slots of the schedule. Although we hadn't budgeted for it, the Lord instructed us to purchase journals and pens for all of the attendees so they could write down what they were hearing from Him (not from us!) during the Retreat.

We asked the Lord about having sponsors for the Retreat months earlier....not to sponsor attendees to come, but to increase overall profitability of the event. He wouldn't release us to do it -- at least not for this particular Retreat. However, just a few weeks prior to the Retreat, the Holy Spirit prompted us to ask for sponsors for the sole purpose to help select attendees come at a reduced registration rate. Within 48 hours we had over $1,000 in contributions, and most of those contributions came from people who were not actively involved in the Kingdom Driven Entrepreneur community. We were able to help several people to attend who really felt a strong pull from the Lord to be there at the event.

A Breakdown (and Revelation) at Office Max

It was a week before the Retreat and we still didn't know what was going to take place in those three time slots of the schedule. We didn't know what we were going to teach, if anything at all. We weren't stressed, but it was definitely uncomfortable. I went to the hair salon to get my hair done and after my appointment my husband asked me to meet him at Office Max. I drove over to Office Max, turned the car off, and was just about to open the car door when I felt a heartache unlike I had ever felt before. I started to cry uncontrollably...the ugly cry...totally sobbing. I didn't even know why I was crying. My hair was looking fabulous and I was in a great mood just moments earlier. All I knew was at that moment my heart hurt....a lot.

I knew it was God doing this, but I didn't know why. The first thing I thought to do was reach out to Antonina. I couldn't talk because I was crying so hard, so I sent her a message on Facebook. What took place over the next several minutes during our Facebook chat was a revelation. The conversation went like this:

Me: Aaaarrrrrgggh Jesus! It hurts sis...my heart hurts!

Antonina: Mmm...start preparing your training for what God has put in your heart. If your

	heart is hurting that means there's a passion there and He's going to use you in the area of whatever He is causing your heart to hurt.
Me:	The Lord just told me that people are going to be delivered from bitterness and unforgiveness at the Retreat...and when they release it and lift it before Him, He will open up the floodgates of divine connections. Glory!
Antonina:	Praise God!
Me:	He is going to heal hearts.
Antonina:	Mmm hmm...I saw that.... the deliverance, the healing...it all ties together.

God is so amazing. He gave us clues. He spoke to both of our hearts and spirits about His agenda for the Retreat. He didn't reveal everything, but He assured us that He had the whole Retreat right in palm of His hands.

God doesn't leave any details out. Before we ever started the Kingdom Business mastermind sessions, He wanted to make sure that everyone was able to fully receive everything He had in store for them out of the experience. Restoration and deliverance was needed to pave the way for the divine connections He had for everyone there. What took place in those mastermind sessions changed the lives of the participants and ignited faithful action, radical giving, and support that has continued well beyond the Retreat.

A New Oil

Apostle Candace Ford was scheduled to minister on Sunday morning and a week before the Retreat we asked her if she was going to be bringing her oil with her. She said yes, but then the Holy Spirit instructed her to get a bottle of anointing oil for every attendee (and supernaturally provided the funds to do it, but that's another story). She reached out to her friend Apostle Lee who makes oils for ministers and asked her if she could get 45 bottles of oil made and express shipped to Phoenix. Apostle Lee immediately started packing away some of the oil she had in inventory already when then the Holy Spirit instructed her to stop and make a brand new batch. He didn't want her to use what she had in store; He wanted new oil...for us at the Retreat!

As she made the oil and was heating it in a pot, the presence of God was so strong in the room that when her husband walked in the room he said "What is going ON in here?" Apostle Lee was praying in the Spirit as she was making the oil and the Lord said to her "Declare this" and gave her the words to speak prophetically over the oil. She wrote down the declaration she spoke over the oil and e-mailed it to

Apostle Candace who read it out loud to everyone that Sunday during the Retreat. What followed is difficult to describe, but it was certainly a manifestation of God's presence, power, passion, and purity. In fact, the Phoenix Retreat was the catalyst for this book. Everything we needed to complete this book was right there at the Retreat. This book was written in only 9 days.

The Only Strategy is to Yield

The one thing that sticks out so strongly in our minds is how God did His agenda, but on our schedule. Yes, during those blocks of agenda time that we were uncertain of, the Spirit of God completely took over the event and once we were released to move on to the next thing, we'd look at the time and we'd be within 5 minutes of our schedule. His agenda. Our schedule. What an excellent, faithful, amazing, and mighty God He is!

Antonina and I will never be the same as a result of that experience in Phoenix. The lives of those who attended, those who prayed for and during the event, and those who have been anointed with the oil we received in Phoenix....none of those lives will ever be the same. We give Him all the glory!

At the same time, we're not expecting that every Kingdom Driven Entrepreneur Retreat will be the same. We cannot bottle up the Phoenix Retreat experience and repeat it for future events. However what we can and will do is continue to yield. Every event we do for Kingdom Driven Entrepreneur will have an agenda that is completely of His design. He is strategic. He's a master orchestrator. He is going to make sure everything we do is going to accomplish His purpose for that time for those people.

We will not get in the way, even when it is uncomfortable and He tells us to do things that just don't make any natural sense to us. Lord, thank You for loving us so much. We trust You completely!

Meet Shae Bynes

Shae Bynes is Co-Founder of Kingdom Driven Entrepreneur ™ with a mission to equip entrepreneurs of faith to build thriving businesses so they can serve their families, truly impact lives, and advance the Kingdom of God.

Shae has been an internet entrepreneur for over a decade and business coach to part-time entrepreneurs and real estate investors since leaving her corporate career behind in 2010. It is those experiences that prepared her for what she considers her most important assignment to date – activating Firestarters in the marketplace across the globe.

Shae is an inspiring speaker, a passionate storyteller, and an engaging teacher. Her life and business were completely transformed through the power of encountering God. She has authored or co-authored several books on the topic of God-centered and Spirit-led business, and she has no plans of stopping any time soon.

Shae holds a Bachelor of Science degree in Computer Science from the University of South Florida and a Masters of Business Administration in Management from the University of Florida. A native Floridian, she is addicted to sunshine and happily calls the Fort Lauderdale area her home. She's a loving wife to her high school sweetheart Phil and mother of two Kingdom Driven Entrepreneurs in the making, Anisa and Nia.

Meet Antonina Geer

Antonina Geer is Co-Founder of Kingdom Driven Entrepreneur™ with a mission to equip entrepreneurs of faith to build thriving businesses so they can serve their families, truly impact lives, and advance the Kingdom of God.

She is a leading authority on small business finance powered by God-given purpose and an abundance mindset. She is the founder and CEO of Simplistic Financials, LLC, a financial consulting company that empowers women entrepreneurs to have profitable purpose-driven businesses that yield more money, more time, and more life.

As a sought after speaker, Antonina has shared her message of financial abundance, simple financial management, and Kingdom driven entrepreneurship as a presenter at Women's Conferences, Summits, and multiple Talk Radio shows.

Antonina was born and raised in Milwaukee, WI and is a Green Bay Packers fan. One of her favorite things to do is to take Sunday afternoon naps. She is a devoted wife to Pastor Larry Geer, a mother to four children and a minister, serving alongside her husband at the Abundant Living Christian Church.

About Kingdom Driven Entrepreneur

The Kingdom Driven Entrepreneur (KDE) community is the place for entrepreneurs of faith who desire to build thriving businesses so they can serve their families, truly impact lives, and advance the Kingdom of God.

It's more than a community – it's a movement! We are activating Firestarters in the marketplace.

We activate marketplace leaders and facilitate divine connections and collaboration through our online community (KingdomDrivenEntrepreneur.com) as well as offline through our live events and Kingdom Driven Entrepreneur Small Groups across the world. We equip entrepreneurs to do business God's way through training, the Kingdom Driven Entrepreneur Podcast, as well as our library of KDE books.

We invite you to join our community and get plugged in today at KingdomDrivenEntrepreneur.com!

Other Books for Kingdom Driven Entrepreneurs

The Kingdom Driven Entrepreneur: Doing Business God's Way (ISBN: 978-0615736129)
The Kingdom Driven Entrepreneur's Guide To Goal Setting (ISBN: 978-0615771892)

The Kingdom Driven Entrepreneur's Guide To Fearless Business Finance (ISBN: 978-0989632201)

The Kingdom Driven Entrepreneur's Guide To Holistic Health (ISBN: 978-0989632218)

Encountering God: A Devotional for the Kingdom Driven Entrepreneur (ISBN: 978-0989632225)

The Kingdom Driven Entrepreneur's Guide To Extraordinary Leadership (ISBN: 978-0989632232)

Declarations of the Kingdom Driven Entrepreneur (ISBN: 978-0989632249)

30732492R00040

Made in the USA
Lexington, KY
14 March 2014